978
Tay
Taylor, L.B.
The Rocky Mountain states

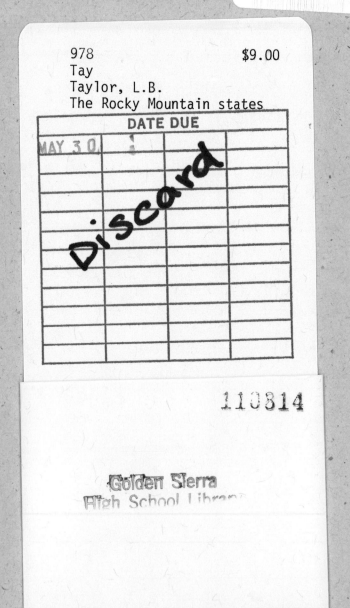

DATE DUE			
MAY 3 0			

$9.00

THE
ROCKY MOUNTAIN
STATES

T★H★E
ROCKY MOUNTAIN STATES

L. B. TAYLOR, JR.
AND C. L. TAYLOR

A GROLIER COMPANY

FRANKLIN WATTS
NEW YORK★LONDON★TORONTO★SYDNEY★1984
A FIRST BOOK

Maps by Vantage Art, Inc.

Cover photographs courtesy of:
Debby Rich; U.S. Department of Agriculture;
Las Vegas News Bureau; Shostal.

Photographs courtesy of: National Park Service: p. 4; Idaho Tourism: pp. 6, 54; Arizona Office of Tourism: pp. 8, 39 (top, left); Colorado Office of Tourism: pp. 11, 39 (top, right); Union Pacific Railroad: p. 12; Bureau of Indian Affairs: p. 15; New Mexico State Economic Development/Tourism Dept.: pp. 16, 30 (bottom), 35, 47; Santa Fe Railway: p. 19; New York Public Library: pp. 20, 24; Utah Travel Council: pp. 25, 34 (bottom), 39 (bottom), 46 (bottom); Denver Public Library, Western Collection: p. 27; Idaho Potato Commission: p. 30 (top); Wyoming Travel Commission: pp. 31, 44, 46 (top); Bureau of Land Management: p. 34 (top); Las Vegas News Bureau: p. 41; American Airlines: p. 48; Colorado Ski Country USA: p. 55.

Library of Congress Cataloging in Publication Data

Taylor, L. B.
The Rocky Mountain states.

(A First book)
Includes index.
Summary: Describes the geography, history, resources, cities, parklands, economic development, and people of the eight Rocky Mountain states. Also discusses the future of the region and includes a glossary of state facts.
1. Rocky Mountains Region—Juvenile literature.
2. West (U.S.)—Juvenile literature.
[1. Rocky Mountains Region. 2. West (U.S.)]
I. Taylor, C. L. II. Title.
F721.T38   1984   978   83-19799
ISBN 0-531-04735-0

CONTENTS

THE
ROCKY MOUNTAIN
STATES

★ State Capital
● Major City
⬤ National Park

GLACIER NATIONAL PARK

Havre

MONTANA

Glasgow

Coeur d'Alene
Kalispell

Missouri R.

Moscow

Great Falls

★ Helena

Missoula

Lewiston

Anaconda

Fort Peck Lake

Glendive

Lewistown

Miles City

Baker

Butte

Billings

Bozeman

Livingston

Bighorn R.

Sheridan

IDAHO

Caldwell

Boise

Mountain Home

YELLOWSTONE NATIONAL PARK

GRAND TETON NATIONAL PARK

Worland

WYOMING

Snake   R.

Idaho Falls

Twin Falls

Pocatello

Riverton

Lander

Casper

Winnemucca

Rock Springs

Rawlins

Sparks

Elko

The Great Salt Lake

Ogden

Laramie

Reno

Lovelock

McGill

Cheyenne ★

Fallon

★ Carson City

Ely

Tooele

★ Salt Lake City

ROCKY MOUNTAIN NATIONAL PARK

Loveland

Platte R.

Hawthorne

Provo

Vernal

Longmont

Greeley

Sterling

NEVADA

Springville

Price

Boulder

UTAH

ARCHES NATIONAL PARK

Grand Junction

★ Denver

Richfield

COLORADO

Colorado Springs

BRYCE CANYON NATIONAL PARK

CAPITOL REEF NATIONAL PARK

Moab

Canon City

La Junta

ZION NATIONAL PARK

CANYONLANDS NATIONAL PARK

Lake Powell

Pueblo

Arkansas R.

Las Vegas

St. George

MESA VERDE NATIONAL PARK

Rio Grande R.

Trinidad

Henderson

GRAND CANYON NATIONAL PARK

Colorado   R.

Farmington

Raton

Lake Mead

Los Alamos

Taos

PAINTED DESERT

Gallup

★ Santa Fe

Las Vegas

Flagstaff

Tucumcari

MOJAVE DESERT

Winslow

Holbrook

PETRIFIED FOREST NATIONAL PARK

Albuquerque

Prescott

ARIZONA

NEW

Clovis

Portales

MEXICO

★ Phoenix

Globe

Roswell

Yuma

Rio Grande

Casa Grande

Clifton

Hobbs

Tucson

Artesia

Carlsbad

Sierra Vista

Silver City

Bisbee

CARLSBAD CAVERNS NATIONAL PARK

Douglas

PIONEERING SPIRIT

The pioneering spirit upon which the United States was founded and has prospered can be seen more today in the Rocky Mountain states than in any other region of the country. Here, farmers, ranchers, and lumbermen are modern pioneers, working with the help of home computers and helicopters. They share an appreciation and respect for the land that continues to attract outsiders.

Whether residents of the eight states in this region—Arizona, New Mexico, Nevada, Colorado, Utah, Wyoming, Idaho, and Montana—live in one of the many modern, culturally rich, and expanding cities such as Denver or Phoenix, or on sprawling ranchland in a less populated region, they share in the captivating qualities of the Rocky Mountain lands. They cherish the beauty of the still largely unspoiled mountains, forests, prairies, and desertland. They are proud of the colorful history of the land and of their ancestors.

One finds in these states a mixture of different people and cultures. Many of the nation's native American Indians, for example, trace their heritage to the mesas and prairies there. Today, a large part of the American Indian population still lives in this area, many on tribal reservations. They continue to preserve the ancient traditions of their ancestors.

The Southwestern states of Arizona and New Mexico combine a rich Spanish heritage with that of the American Indian that can be seen in the architecture, food, and crafts.

Other residents of the Rocky Mountain states—farmers, ranchers, miners, lumbermen, rangers, and manufacturers—still have the independent spirit of the explorers who came to the region beginning in the sixteenth century, and of the settlers who came later from the East.

An ideal climate and setting for recreation and outdoor activities attract many tourists to these states as well. In the winter, there is skiing, skating, and snowmobiling. During the warmer months, there is fishing, boating, swimming, hiking, camping, and sightseeing. The many historic sites, ghost towns, and ancient dwellings are interesting attractions. Many people who come to these states stay, unwilling to leave the beauty and solitude of the wilderness lands.

Much of the land in the eight states is federally owned and managed. The majority of our nation's park and forest land, for example, lies in the Rocky Mountain states. Each of these states, however, has its own unique geography, culture, and history.

This blessed region of the country is not without its problems, however. Such cities as Denver, Colorado and Albuquerque, New Mexico must contend with the air pollution that comes with urban and industrial growth. Then there is the shortage of water, particularly in such dry states as Nevada and Arizona. These and other issues are challenges that residents are facing today, so that the rugged beauty of the Rocky Mountain states will remain to thrill future generations as well.

CANYONS AND PEAKS

The Rocky Mountain region of the United States, stretching more than 1,200 miles (1,920 km) from New Mexico through Idaho and Montana, is an area of many contrasts. The eight states are characterized by arid deserts, steep canyons and rock formations, windswept prairies, and snowy mountains.

The Rocky Mountains, youngest of the nation's mountain ranges, were formed millions of years ago as a result of continental motion—a shift on the earth's surface. Some of the rock in the base of the range is thought to be over two billion years old. More shifts, volcanic activity, and, about two million years ago, the sliding glaciers of the Ice Age helped to shape the Rockies as they are today. Additional erosion, especially by wind and water, created the range's valleys, gorges, and rock formations. The slow creation of the Rocky Mountains is indeed a spectacular story.

In the United States, the Rockies are divided into two regions. The Southern Rockies stretch south of the Laramie Plains in Wyoming. This part of the chain runs through Colorado, where peaks are highest, into Utah and New Mexico. The Northern Rockies extend through Wyoming into Montana and Idaho. The

The Southern Rockies

entire chain of the Rockies actually reaches from Mexico through Canada and into Alaska.

Some of the larger mountain ranges within the Rockies which are part of the larger chain include the Sangre de Cristo Mountains and the San Juan Mountains of New Mexico and Colorado, the Front Range of Colorado, where one finds famous Pikes Peak, and the Wasatch Range of Utah. Further north runs the Absaroka Mountain Range of Wyoming and Montana, with Yellowstone Park nestled nearby, Montana's Bitterroot Range, and Idaho's Salmon River Mountains. There are many others, and all are magnificent.

The numerous rivers born of the Rocky Mountains include the Colorado, Rio Grande, and the Arkansas. A spectacular feature of the Rockies is the Continental Divide. This twisting, ragged seam winds through the mountain chain, actually dividing the waters of the continent. Waters west of the Great Divide flow into the Pacific, and waters to the east flow to the Atlantic or northward to the Arctic. There is no exception to this extraordinary law of nature.

Each of the Rocky Mountain states is divided into different regions of terrain, with the Rockies dominating all but Arizona and Nevada. All of the states are large; Montana, for example, at 147,138 square miles (382,559 sq km) is the fourth largest in the nation. Montana is a mountainous state (thus its name), but with wide variations in geography. The state's highest altitude, for example, is 12,799 feet (3,901 m) at Granite Peak, and the lowest is less than 2,000 feet (610 m). The mountains are prone to severe winter conditions, so Montana's population lives in the valleys where the weather is less extreme.

Idaho is likewise a mountainous state, with elevation levels varying from as much as 12,662 feet (3,859 m) to less than 750 feet (230 m). Idaho has more than 880 square miles (2,288 sq km) of inland waters, and over 2,000 lakes. It also has some of the deepest

Hell's Canyon, in the Northern
Rockies of Idaho, is a mile-deep
gorge carved out by the juncture
of the Snake and Salmon rivers.

canyons on the North American continent. Idaho receives the most annual rainfall of the eight states, with an average of 17.91 inches (45.49 cm).

Utah's peaks and valleys range in elevation from about 13,500 feet (4,115 m) to 2,000 feet (610 m). Utah's lands are rugged, with deep canyons and many rivers, including the Colorado and the Green. Most of Utah's population lives in the Great Basin, with the Wasatch Mountains running along the north. The southern plateau region of the state is arid, with plentiful sandstone and limestone formations. The Great Salt Lake is located in the north central region of the state, and the Uinta range of the Rockies is located in the northeastern section of Utah.

Wyoming is characterized by its large share of the Great Plains region of the United States. South Pass, near the center of the state, originally permitted many early travelers to cross the Rocky Mountains, while most of the range remained impassable. Wyoming is second only to Colorado in average elevation.

Colorado, the highest state in the Union, contains the highest peaks of the Rockies, with more than fifty over 14,000 feet (4,267 m). Mt. Elbert, the tallest, rises to 14,431 feet (4,398 m). There is also a section of high plains in eastern Colorado. While winters are extreme in the mountains, the overall climate is relatively mild and mostly sunny. Because of the mountains, Colorado gets the most snow of the Rocky Mountain states, with an annual average of more than eighty inches (200 cm).

New Mexico boasts a sunny, dry climate. Most of its cities are at altitudes at least a mile (1.6 km) high, so there are cool breezes that provide relief from the hot sun. The elevation in this state ranges from about 2,800 feet (850 m) to more than 13,000 feet (3,962 m) at Wheeler Peak. New Mexico is a state of both mountains and deserts, with beautiful meadowlands, valleys, and mesas (large plateaus).

Arizona is internationally famous for its appealing dry and sunny climate, and many people move there for health reasons. Arizona is most widely known for its dramatic plateaus and canyons, and its vividly colored deserts.

Nevada lies mostly in the Great Basin which stretches into Utah, and, for the most part, has a desert climate. Like the other states of the region, Nevada's temperatures vary according to the terrain. The southern part of the state is in the Mojave Desert, which was long a hindrance to travelers, though modern highways have made travel less inconvenient. While Nevada is mostly flatland, it, too, has mountainous strips.

The Rocky Mountain states are rich in unspoiled wilderness land. The mountain region is known for its beautiful wildflowers and plants, including the columbine, juneberry, mountain sorrel, and lupine. The deserts present many interesting varieties of cacti. The trees of the region include the juniper, ponderosa pine, Douglas fir, aspen, and the paloverde.

Some of the Rocky Mountain animals are deer, elk, antelope, bighorn sheep, black and grizzly bear, moose, buffalo, mountain lion, mink, beaver, marten, otter, and, in Arizona, the burro of the Grand Canyon.

The Grand Canyon, one of
the seven wonders of the world

☆ **3** ☆

A RICH HERITAGE

As far as we know, the earliest humans to dwell in the Rocky Mountain region lived about ten to twenty thousand years ago. They are frequently referred to as "Folsom man," for remains traced back to that era have been found in Folsom, New Mexico. Except that they were nomadic hunters and cave dwellers, little else is known about these primitive tribes.

Far more evidence exists to tell us of the Anasazi Indians (meaning "Ancient Ones"), who appeared during the early years of the Christian era in Europe. These tribes lived predominantly in the Southwestern region of the United States, including Arizona, New Mexico, Utah, and Colorado. The Anasazi, who are sometimes referred to as "the basketweavers," were farmers, who gradually came to live in cliff dwellings. Mesa Verde National Park, for example, preserves such dwellings. The Anasazi disappeared about 1200–1400 A.D., probably because of a lengthy drought.

The next great generation of Indians to appear in the Rocky Mountain region was the Pueblo. Some of these tribes, who built multistory buildings and were extremely advanced, were present when the first white explorers arrived. Among these tribes were the Hopi, the Zuni, and the Papago.

The cliff dwellings of the ancient
Anasazi Indians are preserved in
Mesa Verde National Park, Colorado.

Once-friendly Indians increasingly took to the warpath in a desperate attempt to hold on to their ancestral homelands. Shown here is a group of Ute warriors from around 1870.

Other tribes present during the sixteenth century, when Spanish conquistadores (conquerors) first began their treks into the Southwestern region in search of gold, include the once-nomadic Navajo and the Apache. Further north, in the areas of present-day Utah and Colorado, the Ute, the Arapaho, and the Cheyenne could be found.

In areas of the Northern states, it was the Nez Percé, the Blackfeet, the Crow, and the Shoshone who were first introduced to white explorers during the Lewis and Clark expedition in 1804–1806 and the subsequent influx of French, British, and American fur trappers.

Many Indian tribes, curious about the white explorers as they first began to wander into the native lands, were often peaceful, friendly, and cooperative. Others—the Apache and the Navajo, for instance—were resentful of the intruders. Soon, the Americans' desire for more and more land threatened most of the tribes, and they became hostile. During the nineteenth century, there was a series of bloody Indian wars as white settlers moved west. The United States government, anxious to protect its pioneering citizens, sent troops west to establish posts, further angering the Indians.

The Indian tribes did not want to give up their ancestral homelands. The agreements they did make in good faith with the settlers and with the government were frequently broken, again increasing Indian anger and bitterness.

But, despite Indian efforts, the many tribes who struggled to keep their lands were ultimately defeated during the latter part of the nineteenth century, and Indians were forced to abandon their beloved homelands. Sections of land called reservations were set aside by the government for the tribes, where much of our American Indian population continues to live.

Today, about 700,000 native American Indians live in the United States, many on the reservations. These tax-free areas of land were granted to the Indians by the federal government through treaties. Over 53 million acres (20 million hec) of federally reserved land belong to Indian tribes. The Bureau of Indian Affairs, an agency of the Department of the Interior, acts as a trustee to these lands, but they are, in effect, small, independent nations. The Rocky Mountain states—especially Arizona, New Mexico, and Montana—contain a majority of these reservations.

Arizona has the largest population of American Indians, with approximately 140,000. It is the home state for more than two dozen Indian reservations and communities, including the largest reservation in the country—Navajo Nation. This reservation, close to 3,000,000 acres (1,200,000 hec), spreads into Utah and New Mexico as well. Other Arizona reservations include the Hopi, Papago, and Fort Apache.

New Mexico also has numerous reservations, including the Zuni and the Taos. Montana is the home state to seven reservations, including the Blackfeet, Crow, Flathead, and Northern Cheyenne. In Idaho are the Nez Percé and the Coeur d'Alene reservations, and others. All of the states in the Rocky Mountain region contain at least one reservation.

While reservations today have, in many ways, successfully preserved the culture and tradition of Indian tribes, they are also among the poorest areas in our nation. Unemployment is very high, and education and living conditions are frequently inade-

Right: *Reminiscent of a bygone era, a Navajo silver craftsman does his work. Over: Apache Indians perform the Crown Dance at the Inter-Tribal Indian Ceremonial in Gallup, New Mexico.*

quate. The reservations are highly dependent on funding from federal agencies, and budget cutbacks in the government are severely damaging.

Still, Indians today have strongly influenced the lands of their heritage. In many of the states, a visitor might be treated to displays of the ancient ceremonial dances, rug weavings, sand paintings, jewelry, stonework, pottery, and fine cooking.

Many tribes across the Rocky Mountain states gather regularly for traditional festivals. They don elaborate costumes, and sing, dance, and perform religious ceremonies according to custom. Many of the Indian festivals are gay and uplifting, with games played and stories told.

☆ **4** ☆

SETTLEMENT
OF THE WEST

IN SEARCH OF
"THE SEVEN CITIES"

In the sixteenth century, Spanish explorers were obsessed with the theory that seven wondrous cities lay somewhere in the lands of present-day Arizona and New Mexico. They believed "the Seven Cities of Cibola" to be rich with gold and precious jewels. From Mexico, the explorers made several treks into the southern region of the Rocky Mountains in search of the treasures.

The first white man to enter Arizona to seek the "Seven Cities" was a Spanish friar, Marcos de Niza, in 1539. A year later, Francisco Vasquez de Coronado led an expedition into the region. Instead of finding the glittering cities they had hoped for, Coronado and his men found the quiet settlements of Zuni and Hopi Indians.

During the late-sixteenth and seventeenth centuries, Spaniards began to colonize the land of present-day Arizona and New Mexico. Priests were sent to bring Christianity and the Spanish culture to the Indians, and soon small settlements, including missions and forts, were established. Many of these structures are still

The Acoma Mission Church in New Mexico
is a good example of the missions
established throughout the southwest
by Spanish missionaries in the 1700s.

The Santa Fe Trail as it was pictured
in Commerce of the Prairies, a book
written by a trader named Josiah Gregg.
Gregg made four round trips
over the trail between 1831–40.

present, including the San Xaviar de Bac Mission in Tucson, Arizona, which was founded in 1700, and the St. Francis of Assisi Mission near Taos, New Mexico.

The Spanish colonies suffered frequent raids from hostile Apache and Navajo Indians, who objected to the Europeans' presence. For many years, very few of the settlements were able to flourish.

In 1821 Mexico declared its independence from Spain. The regions of today's Arizona and New Mexico became provinces of Mexico, and trade with the United States, which until then had been forbidden by Spanish rule, opened up. The famed Santa Fe Trail was soon created, as large shipments of American goods began to arrive in the capital city of New Mexico from Missouri.

Soon Americans began to settle in this Southwestern region to trap, mine, and ranch, in addition to operating thriving trade businesses.

In 1846 war broke out between the United States and Mexico over land disputes. The Treaty of Guadalupe Hidalgo was signed in 1848 to end the war, with Mexico giving up lands to the United States that include today's Arizona, New Mexico, Utah, Nevada, California, and parts of Colorado and Wyoming.

TRAILS ACROSS THE NORTH

While much of the Southwest was won through war, much of the Northwest was simply purchased. In 1803 President Thomas Jefferson made the Louisiana Purchase. The land, which he bought from France, included all or part of Montana, Wyoming, and Colorado. This Northwestern territory was largely unexplored.

Jefferson commissioned Captains Meriwether Lewis and William Clark to explore the newly acquired territory, and to carve a route to the Pacific. Lewis and Clark set forth on their expedition from Missouri in 1804 and did not return for more than

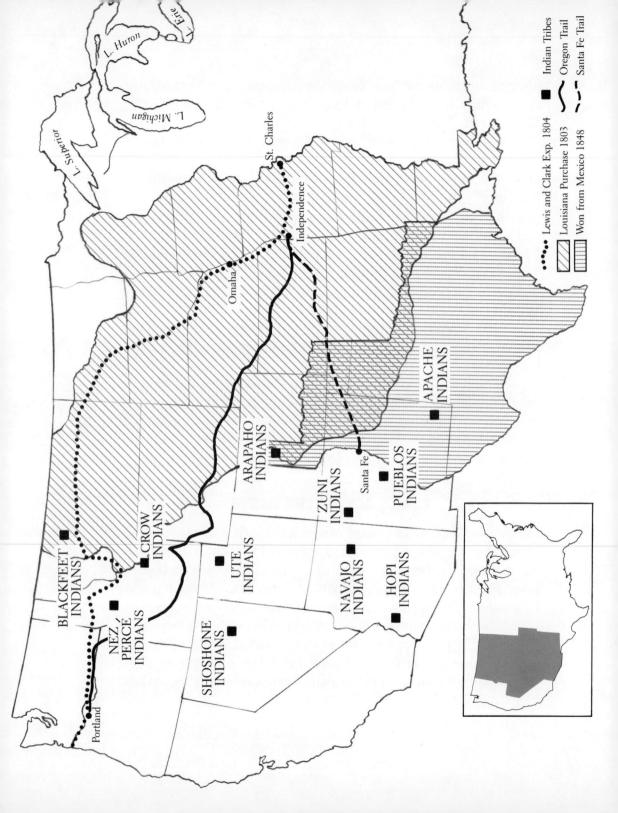

L. Huron

L. Erie

L. Michigan

L. Superior

St. Charles

Independence

Omaha

APACHE
INDIANS

ARAPAHO
INDIANS

ZUNI
INDIANS

Santa Fe

PUEBLOS
INDIANS

CROW
INDIANS

UTE
INDIANS

NAVAJO
INDIANS

HOPI
INDIANS

BLACKFEET
INDIANS

NEZ
PERCE
INDIANS

SHOSHONE
INDIANS

Portland

Lewis and Clark Exp. 1804   Indian Tribes

Louisiana Purchase 1803   Oregon Trail

Won from Mexico 1848   Santa Fe Trail

two years. Many Americans thought that the group of explorers had been lost. Lewis and Clark finally came back, however, with a huge store of valuable information for President Jefferson, including a record of the Northwest's geography, wildlife, and Indians.

This region of the Rocky Mountains was soon visited by numerous fur trappers, in search of the plentiful beaver, mink, and marten. Trappers roamed freely the unknown lands, discovering many of the Rocky Mountain states' striking natural landmarks and regions, and setting up small trade settlements.

THE OREGON TRAIL

The United States was very enthusiastic about expanding westward throughout the century. Many settlers were lured west in hopes of finding a new and better way of life. While many Easterners were heading for the Southwestern region during the 1830s and 40s, others set out for the Northwestern frontier. One of the most frequently traveled routes was the rugged Oregon Trail, which crossed from Independence, Missouri, through South Dakota, Wyoming, and Idaho to the Pacific coast. It was a treacherous trail; many were unable to survive the trip, and some were forced to turn back. The movement of the covered wagons westward, however, continued for many years.

"THIS IS THE RIGHT PLACE"

Another group of early settlers in the Rocky Mountain states were the Mormons. In 1846, thousands of people of the Mormon faith, persecuted because of their religion, left their homes in Illinois to establish a new settlement across the Rocky Mountains. The leader of their migration to the West was Brigham Young.

It took many difficult months for the chain of covered wagons to reach its destination. But when Young first laid eyes upon the

A group of pioneers, in the foothills of the Rockies, taking a break during the long trip west

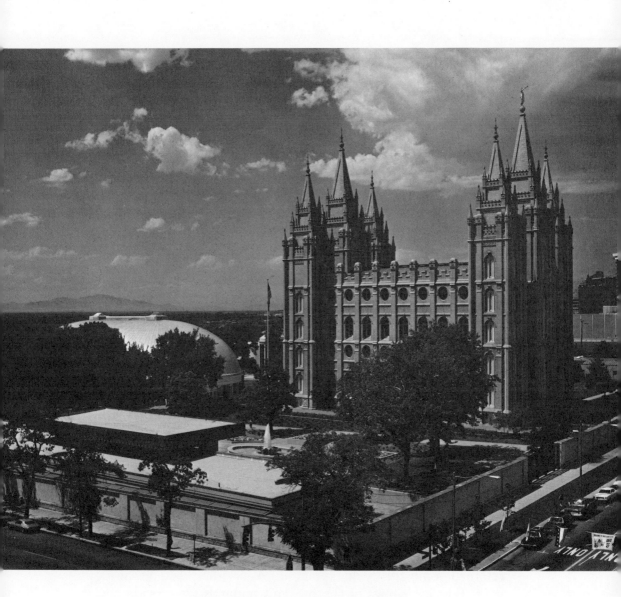

Temple Square in Salt Lake City, Utah, is the spiritual center of the Mormon Church today.

vast and desolate Salt Lake Valley of Utah, he is said to have stated, "This is the right place," and the Mormons knew they had arrived in their new homeland.

The Mormons immediately began to establish their community. A few groups spread out and settled small sections of Idaho and Nevada. Most collected in the Salt Lake Valley, however, and Salt Lake City is still the world's headquarters for the Mormon Church. Utah today is about 70 percent Mormon.

The Mormons were not secluded in their settlements for long. In 1848 the great cry of "Gold!" in California was heard throughout the Eastern states, and prospectors swarmed into the Rocky Mountain region on their way to the Pacific coast.

"PIKES PEAK OR BUST!"

Soon, gold, silver, and other minerals began to be discovered in the Rocky Mountain regions as well. In Nevada, the Comstock Lode lured many thousands of prospectors to its wealth of gold and silver. Virginia City, perhaps the best-known of all Western boom towns, flourished with the heavy influx of miners to the Lode. The city thrived throughout the 1880s.

Gold was also discovered at Dry Creek, Colorado, near present-day Denver, in 1858. In 1859 more discoveries were made near Pikes Peak, resulting in a wave of new prospectors who fanned out throughout the region.

Mining flourished in all of the Rocky Mountain states for fluctuating periods. Of the many flocks of hopeful prospectors arriving from the East in search of the mineral wealth, most returned home greatly disappointed. Many others died on the way west. But discoveries of the precious minerals were made again and again, from Tombstone, Arizona, to Helena, Montana. These discoveries continued to attract people to the West, and many camps and towns were created.

Chinese section hands at Promontory,
Utah, where the eastern and western
lines of the Central Pacific met
to complete the nation's first trans-
continental railroad in May 1869.

HOMESTEADERS

The Homestead Act of 1862 encouraged farmers to move west by offering plots of land at very low prices. For several years, homesteaders settled in the Great Plains states—Kansas, Oklahoma, then Nebraska and the Dakotas—until finally pushing into the Rocky Mountain states. The expanding web of Western railroads further encouraged the movement west. Many of these later settlers, however, were greatly discouraged by the dry climate in some of the states and the huge amount of land needed for ranching. But the influx of homesteaders lasted into the first two decades of the twentieth century.

Railroads were also a great boon to the settlement of the mountain states during the latter half of the nineteenth century. They enabled businesses to expand and aided farmers and ranchers in transporting their goods east.

☆5☆

WEALTH IN
THE LAND

Agriculture, mining, logging, and manufacturing, along with tourism and federal government work, are the major industries of the Rocky Mountain states. Much of the region contains fertile farming land and rich grassland for cattle and sheep grazing. The soil of the Rocky Mountain lands is also laden with valuable mineral resources. These resources have attracted people for hundreds of years, and continue to do so.

IDAHO

This state is world-famous for its potatoes and is the leading producer of that crop in the nation. Idaho also produces much barley, alfalfa seed and hay, beets, beans, wheat, and hops. The beef and dairy cattle industries are significant contributors to the state economy, as is sheep raising. Manufacturing, for the housing and machine industries, and the newer electronic and textile businesses, is an important industry. Tourism is a growing economic activity, and mining and lumbering rank high. Idaho is first in the nation in silver production, and second in lead production. Gold, zinc, and phosphate are also heavily mined.

The rich agricultural bounty of the
Rocky Mountain region is reflected here—
from a potato harvest in Idaho (top left)
to one of the world's largest pecan
orchards in New Mexico (bottom left)
to the spacious grasslands of Wyoming
that support the cattle and sheep
that are raised there (above).

MONTANA

Montana's leading profit-producers are its copper, coal, and petroleum. Other profitable industries are the production of sand, gravel, and cement, and the mining of silver, zinc, lead, gold, and manganese ore. Agriculture is another leading industry, and products include wheat, barley, oats, beets, corn, and hay. Livestock is a major part of Montana's agriculture industry, with the many ranches in the state averaging over 2,500 acres (1,000 hec).

The manufacturing and processing of Montana's many resources are very significant to the state's economy, and there are numerous flour and sugar mills, canneries, lumber mills, and mineral refineries. With over 16 million acres (6.4 million hec) of public lands, tourism is an increasingly important business.

UTAH

The largest industries in Utah are manufacturing, government work, mining, and construction. In manufacturing, the smelting and refining of metals, missile production, and food processing are outstanding. There are several federal defense centers in Utah, providing a significant amount of income to business in the state. Petroleum, copper, coal, uranium, gold, natural gas, silver, salt, lime, stone, zinc, and lead are leading mine products. Agriculture contributes substantially to the state income.

WYOMING

In Wyoming, gold, copper, coal, oil, natural gas, uranium, iron, and trona are mined heavily. Cattle ranching, farming, and sheep production are important industries, as are tourism and federal government work.

COLORADO

Industry in this state includes much federal government work, manufacturing, mining, and agriculture. Products manufactured in Colorado are electronic instruments, film, rubber products, construction materials, and beer. Top mining products include tin, molybdenum, uranium, granite, sandstone, and basalt, along with gold, silver, coal, and oil. Tourism is another major industry.

NEW MEXICO

In New Mexico, coal gasification and the production of solar, nuclear, and geothermal energy are important industrial projects. Defense projects also rank high. Coal, natural gas, and petroleum are important in New Mexico, and also the mining of copper, gold, silver, potassium, salt, and uranium.

ARIZONA

Copper production ranks high in the Arizona economy, as does gold, silver, lead, and zinc. Manufacturing, especially in the housing industry, is important, as is the production of beef and dairy products, vegetables, and fruits. Tourism is a thriving industry.

NEVADA

Nevada relies heavily on tourism, with its many hotels, gambling casinos, and amusement and recreational facilities. The gambling and related industries alone brought in nearly 170 million dollars in 1980 in taxes and fees. In addition, Nevada has active mining, agriculture, and manufacturing industries.

The Rocky Mountain states are also
abundantly rich in mineral resources.
Shown here are a coal-mining operation
in Montana (top left), the world's oldest
and largest open-pit copper mine in Utah
(bottom left), and an oil field near
Lovington, New Mexico (above).

While ranching and farming, the main businesses of the Rocky Mountain economy, are far more sophisticated and scientific than they were a hundred years ago, Western cowboys and farmhands are still strong and independent workers. Work on a ranch or farm is long and hard, and weather and disease continue to influence the farmers' and ranchers' success or failure.

☆ **6** ☆

THE WESTERN CITIES

Many of the modern cities in the Rocky Mountain states, filled with skyscrapers and bustling industry, were founded during the mining boom of the nineteenth century. Others, especially in the Spanish-influenced Southwestern states of Arizona and New Mexico, were populated earlier.

SANTA FE

Santa Fe, New Mexico, for example, is the nation's oldest capital. It was founded in 1610 while New Mexico was a Spanish territory. Santa Fe is located in the Rio Grande Valley in the north central part of the state. The city rests at the foot of the Sangre de Cristo Mountains in the Southern Rockies. Santa Fe has a rich Spanish heritage, and churches, missions, and grave sites are among the historic landmarks of the city. After the declaration of Mexican independence, Santa Fe became a flourishing trade center for the Southwest. Today, with approximately fifty thousand residents, the city boasts a blending of nationalities, including those of Spanish heritage and native American Indians.

ALBUQUERQUE

Albuquerque, New Mexico, was founded in 1706. Like Santa Fe, Albuquerque's early history was dominated by Spanish influence. The city has been a busy one since its founding, for it was also a bustling trade center and a crossroads for travelers. Albuquerque lies on the banks of the Rio Grande, west of the Sandia Mountains. With over 350,000 residents, Albuquerque is New Mexico's largest city today.

PHOENIX

Spaniards first arrived in what is now Phoenix, Arizona, in the 1500s. Indians, however, had lived there for many thousands of years. The city's nickname is "Valley of the Sun." Arizona's state capital, Phoenix is a modern, restful, and wealthy city. Many of its 800,000 residents are attracted to Phoenix because of its resort atmosphere and its healthy warm, dry climate.

DENVER

Denver, Colorado, emerged in 1859 after the Pikes Peak gold rush. Nicknamed "Queen City of the Plains" and Colorado's state capital, Denver lies just 10 miles (16 km) east of the Rockies. It has the largest city park system in the nation. Because it offers a modern, richly cultured city in a beautiful and historic setting, Denver attracts many major corporations and industries. It is a world head-

Among the major cities of the Rocky Mountain region are Phoenix (top left), Denver (top right), and Salt Lake City (bottom).

quarters for coal and oil shale development and solar research. The city is the site of many federal agency headquarters. With a population of more than half a million, Denver is second in size only to Phoenix among cities in the Rocky Mountain states.

LAS VEGAS

The West's "city that never sleeps," Las Vegas is located in southern Nevada. It is a busy, glamorous town, world-famous for its gambling casinos, nightclubs, and entertainment shows. For many years, Las Vegas was a quiet, small town, populated by miners at various times. During the 1940s, gambling was legalized in the state. The great Hoover Dam was constructed to provide flood protection, river control, and water storage for irrigation and hydroelectricity. The city's population and economy grew. Las Vegas has about 165,000 residents.

SALT LAKE CITY

Salt Lake City is the capital of Utah. It is located in the valley, twenty miles (32 km) southeast of the Great Salt Lake, which was first discovered by Jim Bridger, a fur trapper, in 1824. The city was founded by the Mormons, led by Brigham Young, in 1847. The vast Salt Lake Temple of the Mormon Church is located here. Salt Lake City's population is close to 165,000.

BOISE

Boise, the capital of Idaho, is the state's largest city, with a population of more than 100,000. Boise is located in the southwestern part of the state, at the mouth of the Boise River. Partially settled by trappers in the 1830s, the city grew around a military post established in 1863. The post was built to protect travelers of the Ore-

The famous Las Vegas "Strip," lined with
luxury hotels and casinos, is visited by
more than twelve million people every year.

gon Trail, as well as to provide military protection to the new Idaho territory. Today it is a clean, modern industrial center. Boise is also popular with winter sports enthusiasts, for it is located near many lovely sports and recreation settings.

CHEYENNE

Wyoming's state capital, Cheyenne, is a city that has also seen many changes in its history. Once a busy frontier town, Cheyenne's life now centers around the many government defense projects conducted in the area. Warren Air Force Base, for example, is located nearby.

Many charming, though frequently abandoned, ghost towns exist in the Rocky Mountain states. These dusty skeletons of towns remind us of the heyday of prospecting and mining in the Old West. Among the quaint towns still visited by tourists today are Tombstone, Arizona, and Virginia City, Nevada. Virginia City was the largest, richest city in Nevada one hundred years ago. Today, it has approximately seven hundred residents, but the ghost town attracts many visitors with its Victorian manor homes, old-fashioned shops and saloons, and old railroad sites. Helena, Montana's capital city, is another town rich in gold rush history. Nicknamed "Queen City of the West," Helena has many buildings dating back to the 1870s, and historic sites and routes abound nearby.

☆7☆

THE PARKLANDS

Each year, millions of tourists visit the many parklands of the Rocky Mountain states. Each of the states has beautiful and rare land formations, including brightly colored canyons and desertland and breathtaking snowy mountains. Hiking, camping, swimming, boating, skiing, mountain climbing, rock hunting, fishing—all outdoor sports are available in splendid settings.

The largest and oldest national park in the country is Yellowstone. Discovered by a fur trapper, John Colter, in 1807, Yellowstone was established as a park in 1872. Over 2.2 million square miles (5.7 million sq km) in area, this popular park spreads throughout the corners of Wyoming, Montana, and Idaho. The Continental Divide splits the park, which is known for its waterfalls, hot springs, and geysers. "Old Faithful" is the most famous of Yellowstone's geysers, for it spurts great gusts of water 150 feet (46 m) into the air every sixty or seventy minutes.

Grand Teton National Park is located just south of Yellowstone in northwestern Wyoming. Here rise the beautiful Teton Mountains, surrounded by numerous lakes and forests. Grand Teton also has a wealth of wildlife, including elk, deer, mink, mar-

The eruption of "Old Faithful," the most famous geyser in
Yellowstone National Park

ten, and beaver. Together, the Grand Teton and Yellowstone Parks attract many times Wyoming's own population each year.

Glacier National Park lies in northwestern Montana. Sixty glaciers may be found here; the largest of these, Blackfoot Glacier, spans 30 square miles (78 sq km). The Continental Divide runs through Glacier National Park, which has over 250 lakes. With over 1,000 miles (1,600 km) of hiking trails, Glacier has more trails than any other national park.

The area in which Utah's five national parks can be found is known as the "Golden Circle of the Southwest" of the Colorado plateau region. These parks are Canyonlands, Capitol Reef, Arches, Zion, and Bryce. Bryce Canyon National Park is noted for its dramatic rock formations. Great sandstone spires characterize the parkland. Bryce is the home of deer, coyote, bobcat, and mountain lion.

Zion National Park is most noted for Zion Canyon, a 15-mile-long (24-km) canyon carved by the Virgin River, with steep, brilliantly colored walls. Canyonlands National Park is known for its sandstone formations, or monoliths, which are over 300 million years old. Capitol Reef Park is so named because its sandstone formations resemble the nation's capitol. Arches National Park is filled with natural rock arches.

Rocky Mountain National Park is located in north central Colorado. Many mountain lakes, waterfalls, and hiking trails are found in this lovely setting in the Rockies, which runs along the Continental Divide. The park's famous Trail Ridge Road is the highest continuously paved road in the country. Mesa Verde National Park in southwestern Colorado preserves the thousand-year-old cliff dwellings of the Anasazi Indians.

Carlsbad Caverns is a national park in southeastern New Mexico. Visitors tour more than 600 acres (240 hec) of underground caves, carved millions of years ago during the formation of the Rockies.

The magnificent Grand Tetons in Wyoming (top left) and the spectacular vistas of Bryce Canyon National Park in Utah (bottom left). The "Great Dome" (above) is one of the most impressive formations in New Mexico's Carlsbad Caverns.

Another unusual and interesting park is the Petrified Forest National Park in northern Arizona. The trees in this park are over 170 million years old, and have turned to stone, or "petroglyphs."

One of the nation's most famous and frequently visited landmarks is the Grand Canyon in the Painted Desert region of Arizona. Designated a national park in 1919, this magnificent canyon is visited by thousands of tourists each day. The Grand Canyon is one of the world's seven natural wonders, formed over a period of twenty million centuries. First discovered by a group of Coronado's explorers in 1540, the canyon is 217 miles (347 km) long and ranges in width from four to eighteen miles (6 to 29 km).

The Colorado River runs through the basin of the canyon, and adventure-seekers may dare a thrilling trip down the river in a raft. Other tourists hike the Grand Canyon's many trails, on foot or by mule or horseback.

Each of the Rocky Mountain states also claims numerous state and national forests, trails, historic sites, monuments, and recreation areas. These include the White Sands Park of New Mexico, the Lake Mead Recreation Area of Arizona/Nevada's Hoover Dam area, lovely Lake Tahoe on the Nevada-California border, the Valley of Fire State Park of Nevada, and the rugged Shoshone National Forest of Wyoming.

The Grand Canyon in
Arizona is a natural wonder
of unparalleled beauty.

☆ 8 ☆

CONCERN FOR THE LAND

In recent years, environmentalists, residents, and all those who appreciate the Mountain West for its wide open spaces and rich wilderness lands have become increasingly concerned for the welfare of the land.

The Rocky Mountain states are becoming more and more attractive to people wishing to escape the overcrowding, pollution, noise, and confusion of urban settings. Those who seek fresh air and water, breathtaking scenery, and great, open expanses of land have begun to flood into the states. Campsites and other recreational facilities are jammed in tourist seasons. Hiking and riding trails are crowded. Lakes, springs, scenic overlooks, and other park areas are no longer places of solitude and peace.

In addition, the increased popularity of outdoor sports brings a constant stream of enthusiasts to the states. Whole cities and huge resort areas have sprung up to accommodate skiers and a new wave of rodeo fans. Even national corporations have begun to shift headquarters and operations to the cities of the Rocky Mountain states—Phoenix, Denver, Albuquerque, and Boise. Thousands of the unemployed, victims of the depressed auto and steel industries of the Midwest, have also flocked to these cities looking for work.

Scenery, climate, and other such aspects of the Rocky Mountain states' environment are not the only features attracting industry today. The nation's need for energy resources has recently brought much attention to these states. Should the land be preserved or mined for its resources? Much of the land belongs to the federal government—86 percent of Nevada, for example, 64 percent of Utah and Idaho, and more than 40 percent of Arizona and Wyoming. The protection of this land, therefore, is largely left up to the Department of the Interior. Environmentalists worry that even the protected wilderness lands may be opened up for mining.

Coal is a much-needed resource today, and the Rocky Mountain region has the mineral in abundance. While it is already heavily mined in most of the states, increasing the mining of coal could endanger much of the wilderness land, public or not. Strip mining is a frequently used method for obtaining the embedded coal from the land. This method requires removing great sections of surface land, resulting in much damage to the land. While power companies attempt to repair the mined land through replanting, it takes many years for the wilderness to thoroughly "heal." In addition, smoke from coal-fire operations may drift over protected park areas, and operations by coal and timber plants can damage rivers and streams.

The timber industry also poses a threat to much of the Rocky Mountain region. Clear-cutting, one method of retrieving timber, requires laying bare an entire section of trees, sometimes even hundreds of acres. This ruins vistas, clouds mountain rivers and streams, and endangers wildlife in the area. Selective cutting is a much preferred logging method, for it involves only cutting the oldest of trees and "thinning" the forests instead of completely clearing them.

The growth of industry in general is frequently accompanied by a rise in air- and water-pollution rates. Toxic substances released into the air and the region's waterways bring an alarming threat to the area, though the eight states have guarded against it closely.

Also, in Nevada and neighboring states, there is much concern over the federal government's nuclear testing programs. Residents worry, too, about the placement there of the government's MX missiles.

☆ 9 ☆

THE FUTURE
OF
THE WEST

Concern about how this age of technology will affect the Rocky Mountain region continues to grow. State and national agencies and special groups are working on preventive programs and measures. The eight states are protective of their lands. They realize that their resources must continue to be shared within reason, but that many of these resources—prime forestland, water, and wildlife, for example—are valuable and irreplaceable.

Doris Schneider, a spokesperson for the Idaho Health and Welfare Agency—of which Environmental Protection is a division—points out that Idaho is "rigid with its pollution laws, especially with incoming industry." Other Rocky Mountain states have adopted strict pollution laws as well.

Another problem is the increasing competition for water, a resource that is diminishing. Schneider is concerned about water rights in Idaho. There are many court cases pending over the state's need for water for hydropower versus the growing agricultural industry's need for water.

Indian tribes are reviving their claims to water rights in many states. In the past, white settlers often simply took over Indian water sources and systems. Many lawsuits by Indians are pending

All of the Rocky Mountain states are actively
working to preserve the region's
natural beauty for future generations to enjoy.

in courts, threatening water sources needed by farmers and for urban development.

In Colorado, a significant concern is the rise of incoming residents and tourists. "Colorado is a fast-growing state," says Dale Lashnits of the Colorado State Natural Resources Department. "And people have an increasing need for leisure-time activities. We have to meet that need, and set aside areas for the future." Lashnits points to an "enlarged state park system" as one answer. Toward this end, Colorado has established a state lottery, from which a large percentage may go toward buying and developing state and local parks.

"Due to the vast energy resources in the state of Wyoming, there will be more and more competition for the clean air resources," says Chuck Collins of the Air Quality Division of Wyoming's Environmental Department. "More sophisticated control measures will have to be developed and utilized to keep up with industrial competition," he adds.

Collins points out that industries must meet rigid regulations in order to obtain operating permits. "The West is known for its clean air," Collins says, "and energy resources are finite. To date, we've done a good job of keeping industry under control here."

Similarly, strict regulations and routine inspections of the land keep Wyoming's extensive coal-mining operations controlled as well. Members of the Land Quality Division are optimistic that the state's land will not be overcome by mining.

The national parklands, too, must be carefully guarded against overcrowding and occasional industrial intrusions. "The problem with the Rocky Mountain parklands, like many other regions of the United States, is that they are being 'loved to death,'" says Mike Baugher, public information specialist for the National Park Service, Rocky Mountain region. "America is more mobile, and people have more leisure time. . . . Increased visitation means increased impact on wildlife as well." According to

Baugher, each park is under careful study for protective planning.

The ways in which the parklands might be preserved include developing more recreational areas, which, in turn, would lure people away from the most heavily visited areas. Establishing year-round facilities might also do away with some of the overcrowding.

Another measure, according to Baugher, would be to "shore up" the park sites—make them more durable to the wear and tear of frequent visitation. Some park areas—Mesa Verde National Park for example—can be entered only by groups accompanied by a tour guide. This insures that these areas will not be abused. Still, all of this costs money, and plans must yet be made to further protect many of these sites.

The goal of the National Park Service is to "preserve and protect the parklands," Baugher states. "We have to allow people to enjoy them, but we can't be short-sighted. We want our grandchildren to be able to enjoy them as well." Additionally, it is the responsibility of each resident and each visitor to protect the environment, and to be aware of a citizen's obligation to care for and respect the land, water, and wildlife.

The future of the Rocky Mountain states will be one in which the demands placed on the land and its residents will be closely watched. Overall, state agencies believe that, with proper preparation, even with the increased industrial demands of the future the Rocky Mountain states can remain unspoiled. This mountainous area has long been cherished, and it is the hope of these agencies, of residents, and of many visitors that this lovely heartland of the American wilderness may remain just that.

☆ ★ ☆

STATE FACTS

ARIZONA

year admitted to Union: 1912
capital: Phoenix
nickname: Grand Canyon State
motto: *Ditat Deus* (God Enriches)
flower: Saguaro (giant cactus) blossom
bird: Cactus wren
song: "Arizona"
flag: Thirteen rays of red and yellow are in the upper half of the
    flag; the lower half is blue. In the center is a copper star.

COLORADO

year admitted to Union: 1876
capital: Denver
nickname: Centennial State
motto: *Nil Sine Numine* (Nothing Without Providence)
flower: Rocky Mountain columbine

bird: Lark bunting

song: "Where the Columbines Grow"

flag: The flag has two blue stripes divided by a white stripe. A red "C" in the center stands for Colorado and for "Centennial State." A golden ball represents both the presence of gold in the state and the plentiful sunshine. The white stripe represents silver and snow, and the blue stripes represent the sky.

IDAHO

year admitted to Union: 1890

capital: Boise

nickname: Gem State

motto: *Esto Perpetua* (Exist Forever)

flower: Syringa

bird: Mountain bluebird

song: "Here We Have Idaho"

flag: The state seal rests on a blue background. A red band declares "State of Idaho."

MONTANA

year admitted to Union: 1889

capital: Helena

nickname: Treasure State

motto: *Oro y Plata* (Gold and Silver)

flower: Bitterroot

bird: Western meadow lark

song: "Montana"

flag: The state seal rests in the center of the flag on a blue background with a gold fringe.

NEVADA

year admitted to Union: 1864
capital: Carson City
nicknames: Silver State, Sagebrush State, Battle Born State
motto: All for Our Country
flower: Sagebrush
bird: Mountain bluebird
song: "Home Means Nevada"
flag: The flag is blue and gold. In the upper left corner are sprays of
    sagebrush around a silver star. The word "Nevada" encircles
    the star, and the phrase "battle born" appears on a yellow
    scroll at the top of the star.

NEW MEXICO

year admitted to Union: 1912
capital: Santa Fe
nickname: Land of Enchantment
motto: *Crescit Eundo* (It Grows as It Goes)
flower: Yucca
bird: Road runner
song: "O, Fair New Mexico"; "*Así Es Nuevo México*"
flag: The ancient sun symbol of the Indian pueblo
    of Zia rests on a field of yellow.

UTAH

year admitted to Union: 1896
capital: Salt Lake City
nickname: Beehive State
motto: Industry

flower: Sego lily
bird: Seagull
song: "Utah, We Love Thee"
flag: The state seal appears encircled in gold
    on a blue background.

WYOMING

year admitted to Union: 1890
capital: Cheyenne
nickname: Equality State
motto: Equal Rights
flower: Indian paintbrush
bird: Meadow lark
song: "Wyoming"
flag: In the center of the flag is the state seal
    and a buffalo. The flag is blue with a
    white border and a red outer border.

☆ ★ ☆

INDEX